THE **JAMES BACKHOUSE** LECTURES

This is one of a series of annual lectures which began in 1964 when Australia Yearly Meeting of the Religious Society of Friends was first established.

The lecture is named after James Backhouse, who travelled with his companion George Washington Walker throughout the Australian colonies from 1832 to 1838.

Backhouse and Walker were English Quakers who came to Australia with a particular concern for social justice. Having connections to social reform movements in the early colonies as well as in Britain, Backhouse and Walker planned to record their observations and make recommendations for positive change where needed.

Detailed observations were made of all the prisons and institutions visited by Backhouse and Walker. Their reports, submitted to local as well as British authorities, made recommendations for legislative reform. Many of the changes they initiated resulted in improvements to the health and wellbeing of convicts, Aboriginal people and the general population.

A naturalist and a botanist, James Backhouse is remembered also for his detailed accounts of native vegetation which were later published.

James Backhouse was welcomed by isolated communities and Friends throughout the colonies. He shared with all his concern for social justice and encouraged others in their faith. A number of Quaker meetings began as a result of his visit.

Australian Friends hope that these lectures, which reflect the experiences and ongoing concerns of Friends, may offer fresh insight and be a source of inspiration.

As a result of the current COVID19 epidemic, the 2020 Backhouse lecture *Seeking Union with Spirit: Experiences of Spiritual Journeys* by Fiona Gardner, a Member of Victoria Regional Meeting, was presented online to a wide audience on 6th July 2020.

Ann Zubrick
Presiding Clerk
July 2020

Produced by The Religious Society of Friends (Quakers) in Australia Incorporated
Download copies from www.quakersaustralia.info
or order from http://ipoz.biz/ipstore

THE **JAMES BACKHOUSE** LECTURES

2002 *To Do Justly, and to Love Mercy: Learning from Quaker Service*, Mark Deasey

2003 *Respecting the Rights of Children and Young People: A New Perspective on Quaker Faith and Practice*, Helen Bayes

2004 *Growing Fruitful Friendship: A Garden Walk*, Ute Caspers

2005 *Peace is a Struggle*, David Johnson

2006 *One Heart and a Wrong Spirit: The Religious Society of Friends and Colonial Racism*, Polly O Walker

2007 *Support for Our True Selves: Nurturing the Space Where Leadings Flow*, Jenny Spinks

2008 *Faith, Hope and Doubt in Times of Uncertainty: Combining the Realms of Scientific and Spiritual Inquiry*, George Ellis

2009 *The Quaking Meeting: Transforming Our Selves, Our Meetings and the More than-human World*, Helen Gould

2010 *Finding our voice: Our truth, community and journey as Australian Young Friends*, Australian Young Friends

2011 *A demanding and uncertain adventure: Exploration of a concern for Earth restoration and how we must live to pass on to our children*, Rosemary Morrow

2012 *From the inside out: Observations on Quaker work at the United Nations*, David Atwood

2013 *A Quaker astronomer reflects: Can a scientist also be religious?* Jocelyn Bell Burnell

2014 *'Our life is love, and peace, and tenderness': Bringing children into the centre of Quaker life and worship*, Tracy Bourne

2015 *'This we can do': Quaker faith in action through the Alternatives to Violence Project*, Sally Herzfeld

2016 *Everyday prophets*, Margery Post Abbott

2017 *Reflections on the 50th anniversary of the 1967 Referendum in the context of two Aboriginal life stories*, David Carline and Cheryl Buchanan

2018 *An Encounter between Quaker Mysticism and Taoism in Everyday Life*, Cho-Nyon Kim

2019 *Animating freedom: Accompanying Indigenous struggles for self-determination*, Jason MacLeod

2020

THE JAMES BACKHOUSE LECTURE

Seeking union with spirit: Experiences of spiritual journeys

Fiona Gardner

PO Box 4035 Carlingford North NSW 2118
secretary@quakersaustralia.info
quakersaustralia.org.au

ISBN 978-1922332-23-3 (PB); ISBN 978-1922332-24-0 (eBk)

Design & layout by:
Interactive Publications, Carindale, Queensland, Australia

Front cover art:
Drew Lawson

A catalogue record for this book is available from the National Library of Australia

Contents

About the author

Fiona Gardner came to the Religious Society of Friends in her mid-thirties, convinced by the depth and power of silent worship, the warmth and welcome of Quaker community and social commitment. She is part of a small worshipping group in rural Victoria and has been fortunate to be a Meeting for Learning facilitator since its beginning in 1996. She seeks to integrate Quaker ways into all aspects of her life.

Acknowledgements

I want to thank the countless people who have contributed to my own spiritual development over many years. There are too many to name. I particularly thank those who have facilitated, participated in, contributed to and supported Meeting for Learning.

I do want to specifically acknowledge Drew Lawson, who has been my constant companion on this journey, and who has faithfully read numerous versions of this lecture, made supportive comments as well as challenged my discernment, provided nourishment and checked facts!

Robin Sinclair also commented helpfully and, in particular, prompted my thoughts about clarity and layout. Several past participants of Meeting for Learning agreed to share their experiences here, for which I am grateful.

I have greatly appreciated being held in the light by Meeting for Learning facilitators as well as by the Backhouse Lecture Committee members and Friends around the country.

Introduction

I want to begin by paying my respects to the First Nations people of this community and across Australia as the original caretakers of this land. My respect also comes from my appreciation of their wisdom and knowledge, which has influenced this lecture in many ways: in acknowledging the value of naming my own story and background, in making explicit my own stories, in seeing the connections between the land and spirit and in how to listen to the interconnectedness of all beings—animate and inanimate.

What I want to do here is share my own journey in seeking to live in union with Spirit. Although it was daunting, one of the blessings of being asked to deliver the Backhouse Lecture was that it encouraged me to reflect more deeply on my own journey and what might usefully be shared with others. When I look back over my life and my own spiritual journey, I can see much that I have learnt—often slowly, sometimes painfully, and sometimes joyfully. For me, the start of that journey goes right back to my childhood sense of Spirit, my family's religious practice and many other formative experiences. As most of you will know, I have been privileged to participate in facilitating the Meeting for Learning for over twenty years now: a wonderful source of learning, which infuses this lecture. I live with Drew Lawson—a constant source of spiritual inspiration—in a small intentional community, which has also been a place of spiritual nurture and learning. I have worked as a social worker for many years and now as a university teacher, particularly in fostering critical reflection and spirituality for social workers and critical spirituality for pastoral care workers. A continuing challenge in my spiritual life has been how to integrate my spiritual being into all these aspects of my life.

So, why seek to live life in union with Spirit? Such a life, in both my experience and that of many others, is a fuller, richer, deeper and meaning-filled life, connected to that which is eternal. Living in union with Spirit means moving from what is often called the 'divided life', beyond opposing forces to a place of wholeness, to integrating all of who we are in all that we do. To do this means holding together these opposites. In Celtic spirituality, O'Donohue says:

> In order to keep our balance, we need to hold the interior and exterior, visible and invisible, known and unknown, temporal and eternal, ancient and new together. No-one else can undertake this task for you. You are the one and only threshold of an inner world.[1]

Crossing this threshold means coming to know yourself 'in the things that are eternal'—that is, knowing all of yourself, the shadow and the treasure, the egoistic and the altruistic, the strong and the vulnerable, the one who is able to be and to do. Moving beyond and transcending these often-unhelpful opposites means arriving at a new understanding and way of being with doing. Ideally *doing* is fundamentally underpinned by your *being* self, so that all you do is infused with Spirit. This is a lifelong journey. We usually talk of living from or with Spirit, but I have chosen to name this lecture 'Seeking *union* with spirit' to make explicit that what we are ultimately seeking is to be increasingly in union with Spirit.

Living life from this place enhances relationships and work of all kinds, encourages living in ways that are life-enhancing rather than life-denying, and fosters the development of an awareness of what matters—that is, the fundamental essence of your being, and the ability to make active choices from that place. This is also the life we are called to. The Quaker elders at Balby in 1656 wrote:

> Dearly beloved Friends, these things we do not lay upon you as a rule or form to walk by, but that all, with the measure of light which is pure and holy, may be guided; and so in the light walking and abiding, these may be fulfilled in the Spirit, not from the letter, for the letter killeth, but the Spirit giveth life.[2]

This also affirms that there isn't only one way to live life as Spirit. We can learn from the wisdom of others, but, essentially, we each need to learn for ourselves how to live in Spirit. This doesn't mean that life will be free of struggle but rather that our experiences of darkness can be embraced from a more life-giving place. We may choose whether to live in the Spirit, although there are also times when we are not conscious of making choices or are perhaps even unaware that a choice exists. The overall intention, though, is to live in this way.

What I am aiming to do here then is to make connections between what has fostered my own increased sense of living life in union with Spirit, the wisdom of those who have written about the spiritual journey and the struggles and learning of those I have journeyed with. I am grateful to all those who have agreed for their writings to be used and to those many other people who have contributed to my own learning in ways that they may or may not know about.

First, a comment about language: this is a fraught area. Due to past experiences, many people react negatively to spiritual language. What people are comfortable with varies hugely. I will generally use the term *Spirit* to mean the connection to the essence of our Selves, what Quakers would often name as 'the light within'; some would say 'God', others 'a sense of meaning' or 'transcendence'. For me, Spirit is that sense of something greater than the self, which is both in us and external to us, which transcends our being but of which we are also a part. Please translate how I use Spirit into whatever language you are comfortable with. I should also say that, in the examples given in this lecture, the language preferred by the person quoted is used.

I also like to use the image of a journey. I find it a helpful metaphor. The spiritual journey isn't a neat, linear one. It is more common to have twists and turns along the way, to need to turn back and clarify where you are going, to set off in hope rather than always being sure you will arrive. Sometimes you end up in unexpected places that turn out to be a delight; at other times, you regret not being more purposeful about where you were going.

Lecture outline

This lecture is structured according to two main themes. The first theme is what I see as the central pillars, often experienced as tensions or paradoxes of the spiritual journey—being with and reflecting on spiritual experience, the influence of history and social context, the challenges of darkness and light and of love and truth, and the value of paying attention to both our inner and external worlds. Each of these is a way to further understand who we are and the particular nature of our spiritual journey. The second main theme is around how we can nurture our spiritual selves as we travel though life. Here I will focus on the centrality of silence; the qualities of openness, honesty and humility; the recognition of gifts and discernment; and paying attention to the ways of knowing that deepen your knowledge of self. While I am naming these as though they are neat, discrete categories, how we experience them is more like threads of a tapestry inextricably and beautifully woven together. We rightly see the whole rather than the parts, but sometimes it helps to disentangle the threads to see the parts more clearly.

First, it helps to ask what has influenced us—that is, the values and spiritual expectations we have inherited from our own family history and social context. First Nations people understand this: they always begin by introducing themselves in terms of the community and land they come from. So, for me, I was born in Scotland and my family were Scottish Presbyterians. I grew up going to church every Sunday, including after we migrated to Australia when I was nine. My parents had very different attitudes to religion and to the church community. My mother's father was a minister in that church, an emotionally abusive man, but her mother was a deeply spiritual woman and taught my mother the power of prayer. So, although she was sceptical of the organisational church, my mother believed in the teachings and spirit. My father, on the other hand, enjoyed the community of the church, loved to sing and was a staunch defender of the democratic nature of Presbyterianism. As migrants, we found the church was also a place to go where we had something in common with others, a beginning point for being connected to community and so an influential part of my life.

Part 1: Experiencing the spiritual journey

1. Reflection and spiritual experience

Advices and queries number five:

> Take time to learn about other people's experiences of the Light. Remember the importance of the Bible, the writings of Friends and all writings which reveal the ways of God. As you learn from others, can you in turn give freely from what you have gained? While respecting the experiences and opinions of others, do not be afraid to say what you have found and what you value. Appreciate that doubt and questioning can also lead to spiritual growth and to a greater awareness of the Light that is in us all.[3]

The first aspect of the spiritual life for me is paying attention to and actively reflecting on our spiritual experiences. I believe we all have spiritual experiences but don't always recognise them. Paying attention to our own spiritual experiences and learning from them is an essential aspect of living in union with Spirit. For Quakers, this is not a new idea. The Religious Society of Friends began because people wanted to affirm the validity of their own experience of God rather than have this mediated by a priest or minister. Most people would be able to name a spiritual experience of some kind, an awareness of what is beyond the self. This might be a sense of transcendence in Meeting or in nature, or a deep feeling of connection with a group or community; it might be experiencing the presence of Spirit or God within or relationship with Christ. However, most of us feel more comfortable with some spiritual experiences than with others. Spiritual experiences come in many forms in Meeting for Worship certainly, but also during dreams, while walking in a meditative way, while being in nature, at work or during community activities—paid or voluntary—that you are called to do, in relationships, and in being creative. As part of the spiritual journey, it is vital to not dismiss or undermine these spiritual experiences but to pay attention to them, sit with them to more fully understand what they mean for you, and embed them into your way of being and doing.

I want to illustrate this by describing my first conscious spiritual experience and identifying both its influence on me and the implications for spiritual growth and nurture. My family moved to Australia when I was nine. The following year at our church, children in sixth grade were encouraged to sit for a scholarship to help fund their move to secondary school. Classes were held to help us understand the kinds of questions we would be asked. Although I couldn't put it into words, I felt deeply uncomfortable about these classes, which were essentially a form of bible study. It felt as if they were attempts to pin God or Spirit down to words. I feared losing my sense of the experience of God. One day, as I was walking through the small park in our neighbourhood, I had a very strong sense of connection with the universe, with God saying to me, *Don't worry, you will never lose me*. This reassured me, and my sense of unease disappeared.

This was a powerful experience for a ten-year-old child. It certainly prepared me well for a later introduction to Quakers. I didn't talk about it until well into my adult life. It felt too deeply personal and too vulnerable to some kind of criticism or unhelpful explanation. I didn't feel safe that it would be understood and valued. Part of this reaction I think was sensible; it's hard to put into words and talk about some of the deepest spiritual experiences we have. Their mystery is what makes them meaningful. On the other hand, not talking about these experiences means we don't realise what is shared and how fundamental these experiences are to what gives life meaning. My experience in the park also suggests that our spiritual awareness is very present and real as children, but we can lose this awareness as we get older and conform to acceptable ways of being spiritual. Part of the spiritual journey for many of us may be finding a way back.

Although I couldn't put it into words then, what I took from this experience was feeling affirmed in my own direct experience of God and a clarity about what really mattered in my life. I also sensed that I didn't have to accept the dominant way of thinking and being as expressed in my religious community; it was possible to express my spiritual self in my own way. As I became more able to consciously reflect on this experience as an adult, I realised that I had come to take for granted that God would always be present in my life as a guiding force. The centrality of this belief was particularly challenged when I found myself in an unhappy work situation; previously, I had felt led from one fundamentally life-enhancing work experience to another. The contrast prompted me to explore more deeply again what was missing in my spiritual life.

This, then, is the first aspect of the spiritual journey: a sense of knowing, valuing and reflecting on your own spiritual experiences, and being open and active about listening to yourself, to others and to Spirit about the meaning of those experiences. There really is no one right spiritual experience. Your experience may be significantly different from other people; it may be something that would make some people feel uncomfortable or it may be recognised and valued by others. What is important is to know that it is *yours*, to be cherished and encouraged, and to be understood and integrated into your being. It is also important not to compare your experiences with the experiences of others in a critical or judgemental way. Some people have much more dramatic and colourful spiritual experiences than I do; I would say that my experiences are relatively muted, a sense of being with, an awareness of spirit embodied deeply and emanating quietly. There is no scale to determine what constitutes a greater achievement in the spiritual journey as there is more generally in our culture. Recognising this will help us simply be interested in how the experience of others is similar or different from ours. Our Friend, Sue Wilson wrote:

> **Spirit as Bird**
>
> The red-flashing wren dances before me
> a few marvellous minutes.
>
> Experts interrogate me:
>
> Was it black with scarlet back
> or the crimson variety?
> Do you know the wren responds to certain calls that we could teach you?
>
> What I know is this:
>
> My bird lives
> among the rocks, roots and growth at my ground of being,
> following its own rhythm.
>
> I want to stand with a steady heart when it comes blazing out.[4]

A paradox of this aspect of the spiritual journey is that although it is essentially deeply individual, it is fostered when it is shared. Mary Graham, a First Nations elder, says:

> The reflective and questing Aboriginal mind is always aligned with what everyone in the group wants, and what everyone wants is to understand ourselves in order to have and maintain harmonious relationships. The activity of philosophical speculation should not be engaged in alone, nor in a competitive, adversarial debate, but

> with others in a sharing environment, so that reflective thought is always associated with the 'other'.[5]

Drew and I were involved in organising a Quaker weekend camp many years ago. Our small worshipping group wanted more time than Meeting for Worship plus lunch to know each other in the things that are eternal. In one session, people shared in small groups something of what their spiritual journey meant for them, their understanding or experience of Spirit. People were to share only, not to discuss or make judgements. How eye-opening this was! People were astonished and in awe of what they had to offer each other: the differences between those for whom a very real presence of Christ was significant, those for whom Spirit related to the natural world, and those whose dreams and visions were powerful indicators of Spirit. What we all took from this was the richness and diversity of how Spirit is experienced and a desire to know more, not to compare in a negative sense but in the liberation of what could be.

We also recognised though that some people had experienced negative judgement, often those who had a more Christian expression of their Quaker selves. This was deeply painful for those for whom their relationship with Christ was a central element of their lives. One person, who had very vivid visions, also felt judged, perceived as having some kind of mental illness. Asking and expecting people to respect this diversity requires work. People also need to accept themselves well enough to be comfortable with their own spirituality and not to feel judged in comparison. Someone who feels implicitly criticised by not being like the other may react negatively and hurtfully.

The second aspect of reflecting on spirituality for me is engaging with how any experience you have connects with your spiritual self, if you are aiming to live life in union with Spirit. Much of my work life is about encouraging workers to reflect more deeply on a particular experience that has bothered, irritated or puzzled them in some way. What they find, as they peel away the layers of their reactions, feelings and thoughts, is that they unearth their fundamental values, what is meaningful for them about who they are and the work they do. Ian, for example, was upset that his sister-in-law didn't introduce him to her son's new partner at a family party. He felt he was 'not seen, not valued'. This feeling was reinforced by his being a pastoral care worker in a family where prestigious jobs with high incomes were more respected in a society with similar values. Confronting these feelings led him to ask what really mattered, and he affirmed that he needed to more fully integrate his belief that being loved by God and being lovable was what he wanted to live from. This leads to a second thread in the tapestry: understanding the influence of history and social context.

2. Understanding the influence of history and social context

This means understanding how the individual nature of your spiritual journey is influenced by your interactions with others and with the world you live in. Advices and queries number thirty-six:

> Seek to understand the causes of injustice, social unrest and fear. Are you working to bring about a just and compassionate society which allows everyone to develop their capacities and fosters the desire to serve?[6]

Implicit in my experience as a ten-year old is my own family history and its influence on me. All of us are influenced by our family's expectations and ways of being as well as those of the communities we inhabit, including the society we live in. My mother's and father's dissimilar experiences of family and of their faith traditions meant that I lived with the unconscious assumption that it was understandable and acceptable that people experience their spirituality and faith community differently. I knew this was not always so, that there were conflicts between people within churches and major conflicts in communities. The historical tensions between Scottish Catholics and Protestants were still actively present, and the Irish experience of religious conflict influenced my mother in particular. The history of English colonisation partially underpinned my father's commitment to democracy in the Church of Scotland. This personal history prepared me well for becoming a Universalist Friend: consciously valuing all faith traditions and the essence of their spirituality. I needed though to overcome my inbuilt prejudices about the relative ornateness and ceremony of the Catholic, and to some extent Anglican churches, to value what they offered. My mother's separation of the institutional church from the power of prayer, and my parents' differences, reinforced my early childhood experience and belief: you can assert your own spiritual self rather than accept dominant cultural and organisational values.

While these influences were generally helpful for me, unconscious influences can lead to assumptions about life and spirituality that are unhelpful. Part of the spiritual journey is to recognise and name these assumptions. Families, communities and cultures have very strong, but often subtle, norms about what is acceptable, culturally reinforced. Part of the process of coming to know who you are is to become conscious of these norms and to actively choose whether you want to live your life based them. Otherwise, they are likely to continue to influence how you react. Gerald Hughes says that 'when the inner life is ignored, violence erupts in some form or other, whether in physical or mental illness in the individual, or civil unrest within a nation, or war between nations'.[7]

An example might help with this: a woman (I will call her Kate) had prepared afternoon tea in her church community, preparing the tables thoughtfully, decorating them with flowers. She was surprised by the depth of her anger when another community member changed her arrangements to make them 'better'. As she wrestled with this anger, she had an image of her grandmother saying to her as a child over thirty years before, 'You haven't done this right'. When Kate thought about this relationship, it seemed impossible for her to get things right. Her grandmother's assumption was *there is one right way, and it's mine.* This had left Kate with a default, unconscious, undermining assumption: *I am hopeless, I can never get things right.* As we explored where her grandmother may have been coming from, what emerged was a picture of frustration. The expectation for a woman of Kate's grandmother's generation was care-giving at home, not the teacher she had trained to be. Her resentment was expressed in irritation at things not being as she wanted. Identifying the influence of history and social context helped Kate see her grandmother's negativity as not personal to Kate, but, rather, as reflecting a broader picture. Kate could then say, *I can affirm who I am in my context. I believe I am an able and worthy person. I am loved by God, and I can love myself.* This deeper knowing of the self meant that Kate could interact with the world more constructively and raise this issue effectively with the other person.

3. Darkness and light

Coming to know ourselves in the Spirit means engaging with all of the journey. Change is an integral and inevitable part of the spiritual journey: times of both darkness and light, joy and sorrow, illumination and confusion, contentment and despair. Our history can mean that we struggle with being in the light, with accepting our gifts and fundamental lovableness, or that we try to avoid the darkness altogether. Advices and queries number eleven:

> Come regularly to Meeting for Worship even when you are angry, depressed, tired or spiritually cold. In the silence ask for and accept the prayerful support of others joined with you in worship. Try to find a spiritual wholeness which encompasses suffering as well as thankfulness and joy. Prayer, springing, from a deep place in the heart, may bring healing and unity as nothing else can. Let Meeting for Worship nourish your whole life.[8]

The spiritual life comes with a struggle towards wholeness to integrate both the light and dark aspects of ourselves. We seek to stand in the light, and, when we do so, we cast our own shadow of darkness. Part of the spiritual journey is recognising and having the courage to face the darkness in whatever form it comes. The strength of the sun will influence the depth of the shadow: on some days, we might be very conscious of what we struggle with; at other times, it may feel muted. For most of us, this means facing the parts of ourselves that we feel less comfortable with, the times that we act in ways we regret, history that is painful. For some, there are feelings of not being worthy, of not having internalised the love of God. Brokenness can become a fallback position, chosen unconsciously, not knowing that another choice is possible. Writers about the spiritual life also talk about the dark night journey, the times in our lives when we embrace or are overwhelmed by the challenges of the spiritual life. I always feel particularly moved by Parker Palmer's exploration of his depression:

> Midway in my life's journey, 'way closed' again, this time with a ferocity that felt fatal: I found myself in the dark woods called clinical depression, a total eclipse of light and hope. But after I emerged from my sojourn in the dark and had given myself several years to absorb its meaning, I saw how pivotal that passage had been on my pilgrimage toward selfhood and vocation.[9]

For Parker, this pilgrimage was to find his 'true self':

> I now know myself to be a person of weakness and strength, liability and giftedness, darkness and light. I now know that to be whole means to reject none of it but to embrace all.[10]

I am also conscious that the depths of Parker's experience are shared by others, but expressed in different ways. For some, it is more likely to be in outbursts of anger or in experiencing deep fear or anxiety, perhaps having painful memories that seem unrelenting and undermining. For others, the dark night journey can feel more like a time of restlessness or irritability, a sense of just not feeling comfortable. Some people describe their experience as mountains and valleys, others as hills and plains. It is important to recognise, however, that how this experienced or expressed does not diminish the meaning for each person.

Two other aspects require consideration. First, it's sometimes easier for us to see in others what is negative or dark about ourselves. I had an experience of working with a chairperson whom I experienced as pushy and arrogant, not listening to others, especially to me! When I reflected on which aspects of him might also be part of me, I had to acknowledge that my capacity to be passionate, might be experienced by others in a very similar way.

Second, some of us can readily accept and relish the treasure within—the gifts we have—bathe in the light and internalise it. Others find this a struggle: *how can I accept the love of God/of spirit if I feel unworthy?* Depending on what you have taken on board from your own family and community, it may be harder to accept the joys of the spiritual life than the challenges. Drew Lawson says:

> I will allow
> my inner world
> to be untidy,
> without judgement.
>
> I will allow
> the divine silence
> to weave it
> into my divine song.[11]

4. Love and truth

Acknowledging that we are lovable and loved and accepting our inherent worth are fundamental aspects of the spiritual journey. This is balanced with being open to hearing the truth or what challenges our ways of being and doing. Advices and queries number one:

> Take heed, dear Friends, to the promptings of love and truth in your hearts. Trust them as the leadings of God whose Light shows us our darkness and bring us to new life.[12]

Some of us have been fortunate in having a relatively simple experience of being loved as children, which makes it easier for us to take being loved and being lovable seriously. For others, this in itself is a major challenge: *how can I believe I am lovable given that I have been told so clearly that I am not, that love is conditional on being/behaving in the right ways?* For those who have been abused, this becomes even harder. Knowing yourself and believing in your own worth from a spiritual perspective is often a basic and early challenge. Coming from a perspective of not feeling lovable means it is harder to be loving to others.

Love on its own, though, is not always enough to be nurtured into growth. In the spiritual life, we also need truth, but this needs to be truth delivered lovingly or love delivered truthfully. You could think of this as a balancing act, like being on a see saw, holding the tension of maintaining the two in harmony.

Early Quakers were better than us at getting this balance right; they expected to love and care for each other, and part of this was holding each other to truth, to speak what they believed the other person needed to hear. They lived in communities where they met each other constantly, where they met for Meeting for Worship more than once a week and Meeting for Worship for Business, and where they mutually supported each other in many small and larger ways. Being able to name when you felt someone was not acting from Spirit was important to them. John Woolman epitomises this for me. His letters and journal make explicit how he wrestled with this, and how he gently and lovingly, but firmly, would say what he felt. For example, in a letter, he wrote:

> The Truth my dear sister, hath been precious in thy sight and I trust remains to be to thee precious as ever. Christ of old time taught the people as they were able to bear it, and I believe, my dear friend, there are lessons for thee and I yet to learn. Friends from the country and in the city are often at thy house, and when they behold amongst thy furniture some things which are not agreeable to the purity of Truth, the minds of some, I believe, at times are in danger of being diverted from so close an attention to the Light of Life as is necessary for us. I trust the Great Friend and Helper is near thee, in whose love I am thy friend.[13]

To grow, we all need people in our lives who do this for us, who lovingly, but firmly, remind us of the essential questions. *How* this is done is as important as the doing of it. Drew, at one time, felt that I was doing too much that wasn't from a leading but more from the internal and inherited pressures of what I *should* be doing. If, in a tone of judgement, he had said to me something like, *you are being ridiculous, you should work less and pay attention to Spirit more*, I would have reacted negatively and most likely not heard the underlying message. However, because he was able to say with a loving tone, *I am wondering if all that you are doing is from being led or is more what you think you should do*, I was able to hear and respond.

In our current culture, we struggle with this balance. We know we need to offer and/or hear truth, but this is frequently not done constructively, whether individually or in communities. To do this well requires coming back to knowing who we are, being very aware of our own motivations and what influences our reactions to ensure that we are not simply telling the other person what *we* think they *should* be doing. The impetus has to come from and be fed by Spirit to enable us to get right that balance of love and truth. We need to discern the movement of the Spirit within us before we speak. Advices and queries number twelve:

> Be honest with yourself. What unpalatable truths might you be evading? When you recognise your shortcomings, do not let that discourage you. In worship together we can find the assurance of God's love and the strength to go on with renewed courage.[14]

One of my very powerful experiences of two Friends in conflict was that each had their own history from which they were reacting. Each felt they were speaking truth to each other, using that much used phrase: 'speaking truth to power'. However, they had each been judgemental about the other based on their own past experience of also being negatively judged. Each felt their knowledge and experience in Quakers was not being appreciated; one considered the other not respectful of other people's input, the other that the Friend didn't share their own knowledge and experience enough. When they came together with a third person in the spirit of Meeting for Worship and heard the underlying hurt, the history of each other's experience and its impact, they were able to come to a new understanding and acceptance of each other and of themselves.

5. Holding the inner/contemplative with community/social action

This unhelpful paradox is one that many Quakers experience as a tension: Is focusing on my inner self and my own spiritual growth selfish? Given the state of the world, should I not be more active in it? Can being contemplative and praying for change work, or is it simply opting out? Sometimes this paradox is the one that seems to focus most attention, perhaps because it's the most externally obvious: what are you doing in your life in a culture that values doing rather than being. Notice that these are all framed as opposites, as clear choices rather than a myriad of possibilities and a balance that will be different for each of us.

I want to explore two aspects of this. In coming to know ourselves, it helps to be in relationship with others. We grow from being loved, from the challenges of loving truthfulness, from being supported through darkness and light. My own sense is that the vast majority of us value some kind of mutual community engagement; it nurtures us, and we nurture the community. We need though to hold this tension; as well as engaging in community, we need time to be with our own individual spiritual journey—the unique challenges that come from understanding who we are and the family, community and society that has formed us. One of my favourite stories related to this paradox is that of the rainmaker:

> A Chinese village is besieged by drought and unless there is rain quite quickly the village is going to starve to death. They have tried everything they know. They tried all the local people, so they finally decide to send at a great distance for the famous rainmaker. He consents to come and arrives at the village. He asks immediately please build me a straw hut outside the village and give me five days of food and water and don't disturb me. They do this and on the fourth day it rains just in time to save the village.
>
> The villagers go to the hut and drag the man out blinking into the light, give him his fee and pour all the gifts they can upon him, an enormous outpouring of gratitude for he had indeed saved the village. One man came to him and said how do you do it, what is the ceremony you can do that makes it rain? And the rainmaker

said 'Oh, you must understand, you see when I came to your village I was so out of sorts inside myself that I had to put things right inside me and I never got to the rainmaker ceremony'.[15]

Part of what I find moving is the rainmaker's clarity about being 'out of sorts' and the effect that it has on what he does. He doesn't pretend that he is really all right and strong enough to keep going no matter what. He has enough humility to know that he needs to pay attention to his spiritual self, to work on himself internally before he can do anything about the drought. He is also able to ask for what he needs. Most of us usually have some sense of when we are not right within but can struggle to name this. Alternatively, we don't see that we are depleted and what we need to do.

The rainmaker story reinforces the value of community: the villagers represent a community that works well. Your preferred community is not necessarily geographic, although it may be. Ideally, communities are places of belonging, of mutual support and constructive challenge, where your spirit can be nurtured. It may or may not be a Meeting for Worship or other faith tradition. Many of us now would see ourselves as part of more than one community, and being intentional about this helps. Not all communities are life-enhancing, and it can take work to find or create ones that are. Drew and I live in a small intentional community that provides much support for us. Sometimes this has been painful; we have talked about this as being the dark clouds above the house we share. Being vulnerable to others in this way leads to deeper understanding and acceptance of self and others: that what was experienced as annoying can instead be understood as just simply difference and, in fact, helpful difference.

Being part of communities that are loving and truthfully nurturing helps us to get the balance right between focusing inwardly and focusing outwardly. How do we express our spiritual selves in the world around us? Some would see contemplation, prayer and creativity as forces for good in changing the world. Others would believe that change can only occur through more explicit social and/or political action. This can easily become an unhelpful division rather than a complementary and mutually enhancing way of being and acting. Advices and queries number thirty-nine:

> Do you uphold those who are acting under concern, even if their way is not yours? Can you lay aside your own wishes and prejudices while seeking with others to find God's will for them?[16]

Others focus on how the inner and outer interact. Jenny Spinks suggests that it is in being our 'true selves', listening to the promptings of the Spirit and making change in our own lives that we can bring about wider change, if we live a 'life that flows with the Spirit of creation'.[17] Certainly, in my experience, when I am not right within myself, I am more likely to cause conflict in the world. When I am right within, attuned to my spiritual self, I am able to be and act in ways that are more life-enhancing for me and for others. I am more likely to achieve some of the changes that I believe will contribute to life-giving social and community change.

Early in my experience of Friends, I went to Redland Meeting, in Bristol, and was impressed by the desire of a group of Friends to combine a worshipful approach to life with social activism, particularly related to peace and social justice. I was involved in anti-nuclear activities outside Meeting, but I liked how Quakers sought to reach agreement about ways of peace-making, which involved marches and protests, and a silent vigil combined with fasting for a week. I resonated with the way people used silence to ground themselves before discussion and to resolve the inevitable differences about what we should do and how we should do it. It seemed we could then act from a deeper, more connected and ultimately more effective place.

Part 2: What helps with living life in union with spirit?

I now want to turn to what can foster living in union with spirit, engaging with the aspects of the spiritual journey we have explored, asking what fosters a more fulfilling, flourishing and integrated way of living? Much of this relates to paying attention to what is happening internally, but it also relates to taking action to nurture our spiritual selves and asking for what we need. This might include commitment to attending Meeting for Worship or to your own regular spiritual practice. We are also fortunate in Australia to have programs like those offered at Silver Wattle and through Meeting for Learning as well as many activities in Quaker Meetings and other faith communities. Most of us can also access those who are skilled and experienced in facilitating the spiritual journey.

What helps nurture you spiritually is likely to be both individual and collective, and the balance will depend on knowing who you are. What is nurturing will also change over time. A significant, surprising change for me was finding how much I was nurtured spiritually by walking in the forest near where I live; the physical act somehow freed my spiritual self to surface concerns, meaning, sometimes even sudden clarity about how to respond or act, a sense of joy or liberation. Now I build this walking practice into how I live my life. Paying attention to what nurtures you is the key here, asking *what nurtures me, what gives me life, brings me joy, energises me? What practices help me to become clear?*

I am not suggesting this is easy. Henri Nouwen, after being in a monastery for many months, writes of his struggle with sorting the stones from the wheat used to make bread. He wants this to be a spiritual practice but wrestles with his boredom and frustration at the task, until he can laugh at this reaction.[18] Some of the best gifts of our spiritual journey come unbidden, like my experience as a ten-year old. We need to have gratitude for these gifts, to notice and appreciate them, to continue to savour and learn from them. More often, we have to work actively and accept periods of barrenness and doubt where the Spirit is elusive, like Parker Palmer's experience with depression. Sometimes, for example, it can feel as if we sit through many times of meditation or Meeting for Worship and feel unmoved. Then suddenly, unexpectedly, something shifts and we feel deeply connected to Spirit.

Being active and committed to spiritual practice is central to nurturing your spiritual journey. What form this takes will depend very much on you and to being open to what emerges. You could think about the image of a house as your Spirit; ask *what are the foundations, what are the pillars that support the roof, what provides shelter? What is fixed, and what might change over time?* Advices and queries number seven:

> Be aware of the spirit of God at work in the ordinary activities and experiences of your daily life. Spiritual learning continues throughout life, and often in unexpected ways. There is inspiration to be found all around us, in the natural world, in the sciences and arts, in our work and friendships, in our sorrows as well as our joys. Are you open to new light, from whatever source it may come? Do you approach new ideas with discernment?[19]

How then do we find our own ways forward?

1. The power of silence

Drew Lawson writes:

> Silence is not absence, it is deeper connectedness, it is the fullness of God. Silence forms community, brings an awareness of others in difficulty, brings an awareness of our reality, of being loved unconditionally. In Silence we are given a heightened awareness of creation, of our true self and of the Divine. In Silence our goodness is revealed to us, our brokenness too—but this is the lesser. Mainly it is the unconditional Love of God that is revealed, God's unconditional Love for us, and God's invitation to live in that love.[20]

Silence is at the heart of all we are and, hopefully, all that we do. Even those of us who are more extraverted and who find our way to Spirit through music or actively being with people need to recognise the centrality of inner stillness. Some people can reach this place no matter what is happening externally. For others, being in a quiet place is a vital part of this. I can feel the strength of Spirit in my workplace, particularly in facilitating classes and workshops with a sense of vocation. To nurture this, though, I also need times of utter silence; I love the quiet of the Australian bush, the echoing silence. It nurtures my Spirit, enabling me to be grounded in Spirit in the external world. Quakers recognise this, which is why our worship is essentially silent unless someone is moved by Spirit to speak.

For some people, silence is a fearful place, where their anxieties, concerns, painful memories and grief can arise more easily. Our culture discourages being silent, perhaps because of this. What we can come to know is that silence is also a place of healing. For some people, it helps to locate where Spirit is in their body, for others it helps to think about this in a more metaphorical way. Bill Taber, a Friend from Ohio Yearly Meeting (Conservative), suggests Spirit is like having a living stream, a river constantly running through you or with you. Whenever we pay attention to that stream, we realise that it is there. The trouble, he suggests, is that we forget to dip our toes in.[21] Similarly, a Meeting for Learning participant, Diana Campbell wrote:

> Yesterday was a workshop day and so I wasn't able to walk the Labyrinth in the morning. It was a very busy day and I thought

> that, when I returned to the Labyrinth this morning, that it would take me a good bit of time to centre down and get grounded again. To my delight I immediately felt the profound stillness of the sense that I have identified as resting in Spirit. I had not been disconnected from it by all the busyness. I was not aware of it when involved in the busyness and yet it was clearly with me anyway. This is something I hope will continue to be and become always so accessible to me when I do focus and become aware. To know that I am deeply connected and resting in Spirit and that I can go there in a moment on a conscious level when I need to, but also to trust that I am there the rest of the time—I will be open to guidance by Spirit at any time—[a]ble to hear the nudges, promptings and leadings of the Spirit because I am resting in it even in my busyness.[22]

Advices and queries number three:

> Do you try to set aside times of quiet for openness to the Holy Spirit? All of us need to find a way into silence, which allows us to deepen our awareness of the divine and find the inward source of our strength. Seek to know an inward stillness, even amid the activities of daily life. Do you encourage in yourself and in others a habit of dependence on God's guidance for each day? Hold yourself and others in the Light, knowing that all are cherished by God.[23]

This advice encourages us to set aside time for being silent, in order to find that inner quiet or stillness, the internal source of our strength. This means paying attention to this inner place in ourselves. Ideally, this becomes so much part of who we are that we come from that place no matter what we are doing. Marian James writes:

> **The Way of Silence**
>
> I trust what comes out of the silence
> With a naïve trust that it will be the truth
> and that it can't hurt me.
>
> It isn't about words, my own or others.
> The silence will present challenges.
> I will need to wait and be inactive
> I will need to sit with resistance
> To pray and walk
> And draw and write

To expect challenges will be presented
To remember that any challenges have been presented by God
and so I will be ready for them.

The silence is not able to betray me
Not able to lose me
It is a gift—a path that leads to the Truth
The gift of knowing how the world is made anew every day.[24]

Silent worship of course is fundamental to who Quakers are and how we practice. This is where community can help in the spiritual journey. The Meeting as a whole can centre and be deeply held by spirit, even if some of us are struggling. This fosters everyone feeling more connected to Spirit.

With Quakers at Redland Meeting in Bristol, I was attracted to the experience of Meeting for Worship as a quiet, worshipful place. I had increasingly struggled with the amount of words and action in services in my previous faith tradition. In Meeting for Worship, I relished the peaceful way of being though I often struggled to settle into the silence. This was reinforced for me by an experience early in my time there. I had arrived late at Meeting, and given I have an aversion to being late, I wondered if I should just wait until people came out. I was encouraged though, to go in with other latecomers and found myself enveloped in a deep silence that was palpable, nurturing and grounding. Previously, when I had been part of the process of the silence deepening, I had been less aware of it and had had trouble becoming part of it, but coming into the established silence was breath-taking. That experience sensitised me to what silence could be and how life affirming it felt. David Parris's experience shows how the silence of Meeting for Worship can also be a place to wrestle with what needs to emerge:

The Spirit speaking Truth to me through a faithful Friend
I enter the silence and wait for the light.
There is only darkness. Then slowly a swirling kaleidoscope of dark sepia shards. I try to bring them together, to make sense of them, but fear stops me. I try to force colour on them to make them less bleak, less fearsome. But only strong colours appear. Deep blues and purples, crimsons and dark swirling reds.
I dare not steady them and make sense of them because I know that if I do, what I will see will be too awful.

Too awful to see, too awful to face. Carcasses
rotting in the sun; the shame of poverty.
But even worse than that, even worse.

> The spirit speaks to me through another Friend:
> That thing you fear so much.
>
> It is not revolting.
> It is not disgusting.
> It is pain.[25]

Advices and queries number nine:

> Worship is our response to an awareness of God. We can worship alone, but when we join with others in expectant waiting we may discover a deeper sense of God's presence. We seek a gathered stillness in our Meetings for Worship so that all may feel the power of God's love drawing us together and leading us.[26]

2. Place, space and the physical relationship to spirit

First Nations communities have much to teach us about the interconnectedness of all things. Mary Graham says:

> For Aboriginal people, the land is the great teacher, it not only teaches us how to relate to it, but to each other, it suggests a notion of caring for something outside ourselves, something that is and of nature and that will exist for all time.[27]

And, further:

> Aboriginal logic maintains that there is no division between the observing mind and anything else: there is no 'external world' to inhabit. There are distinctions between the physical and spiritual, but these aspects of existence continually interpenetrate each other.[28]

We need to heed this wisdom to pay attention to the physical world, the environment in which we live, our embodied selves. Being conscious of our physical being and the world around us can mean we are more fully engaged in seeking and finding Spirit. The physical act of moving to a different space for silent worship or prayer or for walking meditation, experiencing singing, gardening or cooking as a form of worship, can all mirror the inner stilling of readiness to listen to or act from Spirit. For many of us, it helps to think about experiencing Spirit physically as part of who we are, not separate from our embodied self. You could think about this as *where do I physically experience Spirit?* For example, when making decisions or seeking ways forward, *where is the presence of God in me?* For me this has usually been my gut, but I have had experiences of feeling the Spirit flood my body and flow out through my hands.

We also need to name the connections between our spiritual selves and the environments we live in, our sense of place and what it means for us. First Nations wisdom would suggest that part of knowing yourself is recognising which land is sacred to you and what it means to be with that land. Mishel McMahon, a Yorta Yorta woman, suggests we need to develop relatedness with the whole lifeworld entities of Country and the spirit world, our Ancestors, our family. This is not necessarily land that you were born in or live in but the land that resonates with you, that feeds your soul. It is important to ask about your connection to place and space: what gives you that sense of being nourished? It might be river country with big red gums or rocky, hilly landscapes overlooking the sea or flat, open country where you can see into the far distance.[29] Awareness of this nourishment encourages a mutual way of being with the land, of living in ways that are environmentally harmonious. Drew Lawson writes:

> I am able to see and feel
> the energy in everything
>
> rock, twig, plant, stone,
>   tree, sentient beings
>
> I can see the Divine[30]

I want to acknowledge here that part of the created world is what people have created. You may have chosen where you live because the building as well as the garden or surrounding landscape nurtures your spirit. For some, connections with an urban landscape, with a particular built neighbourhood, evokes a sense of transcendence related to community or shared values. Some people are starting to seek ways of living and housing that nurture their spirit. Others might seek to live in apartments for mutual support, a shared communal space for coming together socially and a shared laundry for ecological reasons.

Much of this is about awareness and intentionality. There may be a particular space or things in your house that foster your Spirit, something that you find inspiring or grounding that may have been made by you or someone else: a painting, photograph or ceramic. Physical relationships with those you love, people, plants and animals, can also connect you to spirit in mutually enhancing ways. Other physical activities too may do this. Part of a poem by Robin Sinclair written during Meeting for Learning illustrates this. Robin is writing about (the many) birds that shared our space:

> Not far from where I sit and write and think
> under a venerable tamarisk
> a bird is perching on the fence.
> Unremarkable and slight, it treats my casual interest
> with indifference. And then it hops and bobs and turns –
> a crimson flash of startlement!
> A red-capped robin. Flick! He's gone.

Each one of these is perfectly evolved to fill its niche.
People are different and fit in more awkwardly.
Down here on the ground
we human beings slowly pace
and think and write and meditate,
trying to find our path.
And all these things flow into us:
the sunlit sky, the cooling night,
the comforting unfolding dark,
the air that's heavy with the scent of eucalypt and honey;
and the warm concern of all of us
for all of us,
reaching out arms to hold each other up.

We find the Spirit here.

And underneath it all,
the orchestration of the birds.[31]

3. Qualities

This brings me to exploring some of the qualities or attitudes of the spiritual life: deep listening with openness, humility/vulnerability, and courage to ask for what you need.

Deep listening with openness

Advices and queries number two begins:

> Bring the whole of your life under the ordering of the spirit of Christ. Are you open to the healing power of God's love? Cherish that of God within you so that this love may grow in you and guide you.

Much of what I have said suggests the spiritual journey is about listening with openness, with receptiveness to Spirit, and paying attention to what is within and without to deepen your inner awareness. This is partly about taking time to listen to ourselves, to what Spirit or the inner light is conveying to us, taking seriously the messages from God, our inner landscape. These may come from something only we can experience—an image in prayer, a sudden clarity, a voice, dreams and visions. Miriam Rose Ungunmerr-Baumann writes that First Nations people call this *dadirri*, which recognises the deep spring that is inside us. We call on it and it calls to us. This is the gift that Australia is thirsting for. It is something like what you call "contemplation".[32]

She also points out the need for patience in waiting:

> We wait on God, too. His time is the right time. We wait for him to make his Word clear to us. We don't worry. We know that in time and in the spirit of *dadirri* (that deep listening and quiet stillness) his way will be clear.[33]

Messages from Spirit can also come from our interactions with the world; the environment we live in; our family, friends, community; the society in which we live; and, increasingly, the global nature of our experience of life. Mishel McMahon would say we need to use deep reflective listening through relatedness with the whole lifeworld: Ancestors, Country, waterways, skies, animals, plants, the elements and community.[34]

We also need to be open to listening deeply to others, ideally in a way that honours how this benefits us, the people we are listening to and the communities in which we live. Truly spirit-based listening is hard work, because it isn't simply about giving ideas and responses; it is about dwelling with the person where they are and hearing beyond words to the spirit of what they are saying and of their spiritual being. Such listening opens out a relationship, deepening understanding of the other and of ourselves.

Humility and vulnerability

Listening in this way implies attitudes of humility and vulnerability. What I mean by humility is being open to the wisdom of others, rather than assuming your way is the right way. One of the more challenging aspects of growing spiritually is acknowledging your imperfections and limitations, the unhelpful assumption and judgements you make. The naming of these opens up possibilities for change. This is a form of being vulnerable, being open to seeing that there are more ways than your way. Somehow, the humility of accepting your limitations is freeing. The other aspect is how humbled or awed we feel as a result of receiving the blessings of Spirit. Our giftedness becomes more apparent as we acknowledge and dismantle our limitations.

Courage to ask for what we need

Related to humility and vulnerability is being willing to ask for what we need. This is one of the hardest aspects of the spiritual journey for many people. In the Meeting for Learning Program, we ask people to find a support group of about four people who will meet with them approximately monthly to actively foster their learning throughout the year before the next retreat. Most people struggle with the idea of asking people to give time to focus solely on them. Where does this reluctance come from? As a society, we stress independence and privacy, being self-reliant. Currently, the emphasis is even greater on presenting a positive, achieving façade. It's challenging to admit that we have struggles, feel inadequate and could benefit from the loving and bracing support of others. Individual family norms can strengthen such assumptions as: *you can do this on your own, you shouldn't need to ask for help*, and so on. Moving beyond this leads to the next aspect of the spiritual life: recognising gifts and using them.

4. Recognising gifts and using them

Advices and queries number twenty-nine:

> Live adventurously. When choices arise, do you take the way that offers the fullest opportunity for the use of your gifts in the service of God and the community? Let your life speak. Where decisions have to be made are you ready to join with others in seeking clearness, asking for God's guidance and offering counsel to one another?[35]

This advice is encouraging us to use our gifts: implicit in this, is being aware of what these gifts are. Coming to know yourself deeply means accepting the gifts you have as well as recognising what you want and/or need to develop. For many of us, accepting our gifts is harder than seeing our limitations; it is like learning a new language. In a class I run, I ask students to list ten of their gifts or what they value about themselves. If they are really struggling, I suggest thinking about what other people might value about them, what people might say at their funeral. Many still struggle, and when we explore why they are struggling, they name family as influential. Family members do not expect to name what is valued but rather what needs to change. They also name the tall poppy syndrome implicit in Australian culture: people should not 'big note' themselves.

What is experienced as a gift to one person may be a challenge to another. One person's gift for organisational detail may be seen by another as irritating; alternatively, a person's capacity to generate new possibilities for action might be seen by another as frustratingly unrealistic. Calvi suggests that sometimes we may miss the subtlety of a particular gift:

> If we try to be too particular in seeking understanding of having a gift, we may miss the broad scope a gift may offer. We may frustrate ourselves by asking for a job description when what we really need to learn next is a change of tone.[36]

Finding a vocation is another way people think about this; not just a vocation in the sense of work. Alphonso asks, what is my life vocation? What is my fundamental way of being or orientation to the world, my <u>being</u> vocation as opposed to my <u>doing</u> vocation? Am I essentially a person who has the capacity to be present, to sit with others; am I someone whose vocation is to be practical or to inspire others to see the world differently?[37] This opens up possibilities for how this can then be expressed. One participant after Meeting for Learning said:

> Through building a connection with the Spirit in myself and others, I was prompted to share my gifts. I felt led to discover my voice in singing, in ministry, in leading epilogue and in facilitating a massage and gentle exercise time.[38]

A useful question, then, might be *where are my gifts and energies best used?* Some might seek change in relationships, others change in community, and broader. The question is *what is life-enhancing here? How can I use my gifts to bring about great flourishing for myself and for others?* The next question then is *how do we do this: how do we discern the way forward?*

5. Active discernment

If you are seeking to live your life in union with Spirit, this means constant discerning of where you are being led and paying attention to your inner self for clarity about the way forward. This might mean asking yourself questions such as *where am I being led? Where is God for me here? What is being asked of me? Where am I most fully myself? How do I make sure that I am being led by Spirit and not by my own ego or my own desires or fears?* Quakers use the word 'leading' a lot. Others might ask *what am I being called to?* Both have a sense of yearning for me, the desire to follow Spirit, if we could only work out what that means.

Engaging with these questions can mark moving from seeing Meeting for Worship as something you *do*—that is, a time of the week that you devote to the spiritual experience—to living your life in union with Spirit. The hope in the spiritual journey is that your ability to do this will grow so that discernment of Spirit becomes integral to who you are. Helen Bayes says:

> Discernment is the conscious, prayerful discipline we can (must, in fact) follow to find clarity about openings, different paths or timing, and to guard against self-interest on the one hand and human scepticism on the other. It is about paying attention to God's guidance, not about taking control ourselves.[39]

Sometimes we assume that discernment is only about the bigger decisions of life: *should I change jobs, move house, commit to a new relationship?* It can seem to be a matter of deciding between a right and wrong or good and bad decision, but it can often be between two goods. One of my hardest discernments was deciding which of the things I loved to do had to go; there were simply too many of them. The processes can apply usefully to all aspects of life. Ideally, this would be so much a part of who we are that we would almost do it without needing to make a conscious decision. Smaller discernments can fit into larger ones. You might, for example, have decided as part of your commitment to simplicity to live in a more sustainable way. You feel a sense of rightness about this decision. This is followed though by daily small discernments: *what do I eat? Do I drive or ride my bicycle? Do I not have a cup of coffee because I forgot my reusable cup?*

Drew Lawson has looked at the traditional Quaker ways of wrestling with discernment. He suggests four categories that I find helpful.[40] First, there is the bother: I have a sense of unease about something, perhaps I should be doing something about it or I should be getting other people to see that this needs to be done. 'Should' words are a good sign that it is a bother, rather than a leading. Next is a **leading**, a call from God that is accepted and acted upon, a calm willingness to take a risk even if I feel some trepidation. This might be something simple, like ministering in Meeting for Worship or taking on a task in Meeting. A greater degree of leading is a **concern**, a call from God that requires me to change my way of living. This has a greater degree of certainty and often joy and clarity, which may be combined with some doubt. Finally, a **necessity** is an insistent call about which I have no choice, which becomes an integral part of life, something necessary for life. Sometimes what starts as a bother or a concern can become a necessity: daily spiritual practice might begin as something I feel I should do, become something I feel I need to do, develop into something that enhances my life and finally becomes something I can't live without.

Often a leading has a feeling of inner rightness about it. When I look back over my working life, I can see that, when I paid attention to this, I took on work that was much more satisfying and in tune with my spiritual self. I was fortunate early in my life that such jobs just appeared. Then I was in a job that ended before I was ready: there was a change of government, and the new government didn't see the relevance of consumer advocacy. I was very grateful to be offered a new job in an agency that philosophically seemed to fit with my values. Over time, though, I came to realise that I didn't have that sense of inner rightness there; I had taken the job in flight rather than taking time to discern. The work itself was worthwhile and valued, but it wasn't the right place for me. Fortunately, another job opened up, which did have that feeling of inner rightness. We don't always have that choice, but perhaps we would do so more often if we asked the question: *is this fitting with where I am led?*

What does this sense of inner rightness or clarity of discernment feel like? It isn't the same for everyone, and you need to tune into how this is expressed for you. Generally, the kind of feeling is of dawning clarity or certainty, even if it is intermittently clouded by doubts. It might be reinforced by a physical sense of relief, of your body relaxing, or of an affirming weightiness in your abdomen or heart. You might feel filled with joy or exhilaration. If it isn't a leading, on the other hand, you are more likely to feel a sense of anxiety, irritation or doubt, unease or discomfort; you might physically feel restless, tired or lacking in energy.

We are fortunate as Quakers to have helpful processes related to discernment: we practice this collectively in Business Meetings seeking ways forward. We talk about seeking the movement of the spirit, affirming that this is a useful and valid way to make decisions. This enables movement beyond the either/or of much decision-making to more transformative choices. These processes can be used in Clearness Meetings, where a group discerns together the way forward about a particular question, issue or conflict for an individual, group or community. For individual Clearness Meetings, people can choose who they think will be most helpful. Making these work comes back to knowing yourself, being able to see what your preferences and reactions are and not imposing them on others. This can be difficult to do: we can be so sure about what would be better for the Meeting or for the person. A Clearness Meeting works best when the person is helped by the group in the spirit of Meeting for Worship, so that the questions they ask and comments they make are Spirit led, rather than ego led.

6. Being intentional: Connecting with spirit

This brings me full circle to saying that each of us needs to know ourselves in the things that are eternal, to recognise what particularly feeds our soul and to be actively engaged in what fosters our spiritual life. I used to have the naïve view that if I attended Quaker Meeting for Worship and followed leadings, all would be well in my spiritual life. While I had indeed experienced times of darkness, I had always felt that God was present. In my mid-thirties, for a mix of reasons—a combination of what was happening at work and in our small community—I felt I had lost my way. Part of what emerged was the need to be more intentional about nurturing my spiritual being.

There are many ways to do this, and many people have written about them, so I will explore some only briefly here. Returning to where I began this lecture, what is important is to know yourself and to be open to how your spiritual journey will change over time. What is consistent is the need to be **faithful** and **actively intentional**. We know that to do any other aspect of our life well, we need to learn and to practise. Spiritual strength, spiritual muscles also need development and work to be maintained and extended.

So what might some of these be?

A common theme in the spiritual life is the **intentional use of journals**. Howard Brinton points out that Quakers have frequently used religious autobiography, usually called a 'journal' to write about their spirituality, given that it is based on personal experience rather than formal creeds.[41] You can use journaling as a way of paying attention, ideally something that only you will read unless you choose otherwise. Such writing can help clarify understanding, remind you of learning, and be a space to name what you might be uncomfortable about saying to someone else. Catherine Heywood decided to use journaling as way of paying more attention to her experience in Meeting for Worship:

> I am struck now by what I knew then, without realising it. I am also struck by the power of this reflective journaling which enables the hidden to become more accessible. ... When I re-read this next extract from my journal, I wondered how I could have forgotten it, for the experience was very powerful.[42]

Obviously, you can journal about anything, so I have started with this because you can then apply it to all of the other possible ways of being intentional.

A second theme is **committing yourself to attending workshops or activities** that you think may influence your spiritual journey or that you feel nudged to go to even if you aren't sure why. Sometimes this might require you to generate the kind of activities or engagement that you need with others.

My youth group experience was significant for my spiritual development: I could see that I was better at some things than others. It wasn't a competitive environment; the culture was one of acceptance of differences that contributed to a positive sense of myself. In my late teens, I went to a weekend focused on understanding yourself from a spiritual perspective. To my surprise, people who seemed much older and wiser than I was (probably in their thirties!) talked about their vulnerabilities, limitations, and regrets about opportunities missed. This was an eye-opener for me, the kind of experience we all need to recognise that we all struggle.

In Australia, we have Quaker Learning Australia with the Meeting for Learning Program, and Silver Wattle offers a wide range of retreats or workshops that meet differing spiritual needs and preferences. Other faith traditions also offer teachings and retreats: for example, Buddhist meditation, Catholic, silent and led retreats. More people are now offering some kind of spiritual guidance or spiritual direction. Making an active commitment to these can be a significant internal shift in commitment to union with spirit. Because there is such a wide variety, you can choose what feels right for where you are at a particular time. This can mean overcoming your own internal expectations of being able to do this for yourself and recognising the experience and wisdom of others. Jim Newell, a Victorian Friend, used to say that Quakers welcome you in and assume you will know how to worship. This can reflect our unwillingness, David Johnson suggests,

> to give over, to submit to any person in their spiritual growth even for a time, as if it is not possible to use someone else's experience and knowledge and one's own discernment to test for the Spirit.[43]

Sometimes you need to be active or intentional in creating the kinds of opportunities you need. For example, as relatively isolated Friends, Drew and I were once part of a group of nine people that had a fifteen-minute Meeting for Worship at a set time each night. This was important, I think, for all of us to feel connected in the Spirit. Initiating an annual weekend primarily for Friends from rural Meetings was also a significant aspect of us feeling linked to Friends and to deepening our spiritual journey. For others, this might be about forming a spiritual friendship, committing to meeting regularly to worship together and/or to explore where they are with Spirit.

It might be about organising a midweek Meeting for Worship for those who want to meet more often or about finding a support group for seeking socially just change.

Some experiences that you feel led to may appear tangential to the spiritual journey, but **anything that fosters knowing yourself more deeply is a part of this**. I found it very helpful to attend workshops on personality difference. Margaret Dwyer, a Sister of Charity, led workshops on Myers Briggs typology, including how personality connected to preferred ways of worshipping.[44] The aim was deeper acceptance of the self as part of moving to wholeness. This typology made sense to me; what a relief it was to discover that my need for quiet and to read to regenerate was now wholly understandable and could be guilt free! This was reinforced later when I completed an Enneagram workshop with Margaret. This again meant sitting with *who am I, where do I fit here? How can I recognise and name what is distinct about me, though of course shared to some degree with others?* Part of the challenge of the Enneagram is that it requires you to identify your particular Achilles heel, the aspect of you that is often your downfall in relationships—for example, seeking perfection or avoiding decisions.

Some people feel that such typologies are based on psychology rather than spiritually based. However, people such as Margaret Dwyer point out that the spiritual life is about accepting not only the gifts and strengths we have from who we are but also the challenges and limitations. To grow spiritually, we need to recognise and affirm both; and such typologies can help make these conscious.

Although the aim is to live all of life in union with Spirit, in moving towards achieving this aim it is important to commit to regular spiritual practice, preferably daily. For some people, this might be daily prayer or meditation, whether sitting or walking. I have known people to get up before sunrise and walk on the beach to begin the day from Spirit or to use the time before children were up to sit in a favoured space in their house or garden to meditate. Others use painting or drawing: Wilma Davidson attended a contemplative retreat where a participant mentioned painting a mandala a day. Wilma started this activity at a Meeting for Learning retreat, and the practice grew, so that she made mandala cards for people at significant points in their lives. She says:

> In the making of these cards I felt more like the channel than the creator. The feeling I had was that same feeling suggested to be applied to spoken ministry—that we 'can't not' share our ministry. The whole process was to me a truly mystical experience. And not only is it such fun, but I come away at the end of a painting session feeling peaceful and complete.[45]

When you start a spiritual practice, be realistic; don't say you will do thirty minutes if you know you are likely to do only five. Build up over time rather than start too optimistically and have it not work.

Next, pay attention to what happens for you in other unconscious ways. Carl Jung's book *Memories, Dreams and Reflections* explores how each of these can bring to awareness something influencing you unconsciously.[46] Dreams continue to give me useful information about what I am really feeling or where I am being led. At one stage in my working life, I was offered the chance to act in a senior role while my manager was away for several months. I dreamed that I had arrived in prison, and the prison governor, someone I had worked with previously, greeted me enthusiastically in my new role as a prisoner. He told me he had arranged for me to work in the prison library because I loved to read. I was grateful but still uncomfortable being in prison. As I explored this dream, I realised it was telling me that this senior role would feel like being in prison. Some things I liked about the role—symbolised by the library—but nonetheless, it would still feel like a prison. This clarified for me the 'shoulds' I had about the job: *I should be grateful to be considered; I should be willing to help out.* I suggested that two of us could share the role, and that felt manageable for us both.

Like David Parris, I do also occasionally have experiences in Meeting for Worship that bring to the light something that needs to be noticed: a memory, a feeling or a thought that is uncomfortable, or the challenge of accepting a quality I haven't recognised. Being held in the silence of Meeting can be a very powerful place to allow these to emerge and perhaps move to a new place of acceptance or understanding.

At other times, it is possible to have an image arise while you are doing something else, such as walking through the bush or gardening, or suddenly a feeling of certainty or clarity is present, sometimes quite physically. I occasionally hear what I experience as the voice of God or Spirit, sometimes in Meeting for Worship, but more often when walking in nature. Sometimes this is prompted by walking with a question or walking when I am conscious that a question is floating around for me. Others have visions of religious figures or of the cosmos, which can be very dramatic—sometimes to ensure that we take heed of them. These can feel alarming: our culture is so much about rationality that suddenly hearing a voice or being dazzled by an image can be troubling. It is useful to ask yourself, *is this helpful for my spiritual self; is this illuminating in some way or even simply reassuring or comforting?* Not everything can be explained rationally, and not everything is clear immediately. Sometimes you are presented with something that you simply have to sit with. Journaling about this, including making images, can help you engage with the experience. Again, this is not a process that occupies only your rational self; you might usefully take this into prayer or meditation.

Another sign of the unconscious can be your reaction to others: a strong reaction is often a sign that there is something for you to learn about yourself. It is useful to ask *what is going on here? Why am I feeling irritated, annoyed, puzzled?* Again, you can journal about this or take it into Meeting for Worship or your own prayer or mediation time.

Embedding the spiritual in the everyday is part of this. Drew Larson writes:

> may I engage in the everyday
> as part of my spiritual practice.[47]

We inhabit a world generally not attuned to the spiritual life. Our political, cultural and social systems are geared to other norms, whether in work or caring for children or others, from what we eat to what clothes we can buy and how we deal with our rubbish. If we are aiming to live in union with Spirit, there is a sense of constantly having to engage with different expectations and to ask *how do I engage with these? When do I accept what is or change my attitude towards it? And when do I seek to change it? How do I balance ensuring that my own wellbeing is cared for while I'm caring for the people and environment around me?*

Much of this comes back to nurturing your own spiritual self, combined with constant discernment, asking, where am I now? How do I express this now? Am I coming from a grounded place so that my attitude to what I am doing is based on my spiritual self? It is about moving to the point where you see that who you are spiritually is your being self, not simply your doing self, the self that you tune into and live from. Small things can help with this, provided you are doing the overall work to nurture your self. For example, I like to make sure I am grounded before I go to a class. This often takes a very short time: a minute or less. Sometimes if I have been engaged in something contentious, it might take longer. It's about focusing inwardly, letting go of what I have been doing and tuning into where I would physically locate my spiritual self. I will use the time of walking to a class or, if necessary, make the excuse of going to the toilet to ensure a quiet space. People have different ways of developing their ability to do this: using a stone in their pocket to remind them, having an image on their desk, wearing a ring or bracelet. For some people, having a daily practice of meditation or prayer to start the day orients them to come from their being self through the day. The more you practice, the more embedded this will become in simply being who you are.

> I acknowledge the bridges I have crossed
> into new spiritual countries
>
> I will now burn the bridges for there is no going back.[48]

I want to finish by returning to my own spiritual roots with what feels like a heartfelt cry from the Celtic book of prayer:

> Why is there so little anxiety to get time to pray? Why is there so little forethought in the laying out of time and employment so as to secure a large portion of each day for prayer? Why is there so much speaking, yet so little prayer? Why is there so much running to and fro, yet so little prayer? ...
>
> In one single quiet hour of prayer [the soul] will often make more progress than in days of company with others. It is in the desert that dew falls freshest and the air is purest. So with the soul. It is when none but God is nigh; ... like the desert air in which there is mingled no noxious breath of man, surrounds and pervades the soul; it is then that the eye gets the clearest, simplest view of eternal certainties; it is then that the soul gathers in wondrous refreshment and power and energy.
>
> And so it is also in this way that we become truly useful to others. It is when coming out fresh from communication with God that we go forth to ... work successfully.[49]

Endnotes

[1] J O'Donohue, *Anam Cara: Spiritual Wisdom from the Celtic World*, Bantam Books, Sydney, 1999, p. 14.

[2] Elders at Balby, *Handbook of Quaker Practice and Procedure in Australia*, 6th edn. Yearly Meeting of the Religious Society of Friends (Quakers), Australia, 2005, p. 18.

[3] Religious Society of Friends (Quakers) Australia, Advices and queries number five, *Advices and Queries: A Compilation of Australian and British Advices and Queries*. Religious Society of Friends (Quakers) in Australia, 2009.

[4] S Wilson https://australianfriend.org/three-poems-2/

[5] M Graham, 'Some Thoughts about the Philosophical Underpinnings of Aboriginal Worldviews', *Worldviews: Environment, Culture, Religion*, vol. 3, no 2, 1999, p. 108.

[6] Religious Society of Friends (Quakers) Australia, Advices and queries number thirty-six.

[7] G Hughes, *God of Surprises*, Paulist Press, New York, 1985, p. 132.

[8] Religious Society of Friends (Quakers) Australia, Advices and queries number eleven.

[9] PJ Parker, *Let Your Life Speak: Listening for the Voice of Vocation*, John Wiley and Sons, San Francisco, 2000, pp. 56-7.

[10] PJ Parker, *Let Your Life Speak*, p. 70.

[11] D Lawson, *Mystical Meadows*, Whipstick Publications No 2, Bendigo, 2017, p. 151.

[12] Religious Society of Friends (Quakers) Australia, Advices and queries number one.

[13] J Woolman, in *Meeting for Learning Resource Manual*. Australia Yearly Meeting, Australia, 2018-2019, p. 44.

[14] Religious Society of Friends (Quakers) Australia, Advices and queries number twelve.

[15] CG Jung, *The Collected Works of C. G. Jung*, Vol 14. p. 419-20, Bollingen Series, Princeton University Press, 1976, pp. 419-420. NB this version adapted by Robert Johnson.

[16] Religious Society of Friends (Quakers) Australia, Advices and queries number thirty-nine.

[17] J Spinks, *Support for Our True Selves: Nurturing the Space Where Leadings Flow*, James Backhouse Lecture, 2007, p. 49.

[18] H Nouwen, *The Genesee Diary Report from a Trappist Monastery*, Image Books, Garden City, NY, 1981.

[19] Religious Society of Friends (Quakers) Australia, Advices and queries number seven.

[20] D Lawson, quoted in *Meeting for Learning Resource Manual*, p. 134.

[21] W Taber, *Four Doors to Meeting for Worship*, Pendle Hill Pamphlet #306, Pendle Hill Publications, Wallingford, 1992.

[22] D Campbell, personal communication, 2019.

[23] Religious Society of Friends (Quakers) Australia, Advices and queries, number three.

[24] M James, quoted in *Meeting for Learning Resource Manual*, p. 130.

[25] D Parris, quoted in *Meeting for Learning Resource Manual*, p. 104.

[26] Religious Society of Friends (Quakers) Australia, Advices and queries, number nine.

[27] Graham, 'Some Thoughts about the Philosophical Underpinnings of Aboriginal Worldviews', p. 108.

[28] Graham, 'Some Thoughts about the Philosophical Underpinnings of Aboriginal Worldviews', p. 113.

[29] M McMahon, training and personal communication, 2019.

[30] D Lawson, *Mystical Meadows*, p. 135.

[31] R Sinclair, shared at Meeting for Learning, 2019.

[32] M R Ungunmerr-Baumann, Dadirri: Inner Deep Listening. https://www.miriamrosefoundation.org.au/images/Dadirri_Handout.pdf, p. 1.

[33] Ungunmerr-Baumann, Dadirri, p. 3.

[34] M McMahon, 'Lotjpa-nhanuk: Indigenous Australian child-rearing discourses', PhD thesis, La Trobe University, 2017.

[35] Religious Society of Friends (Quakers) Australia, Advices and queries, number twenty-nine.

[36] J Calvi, 'Having a Gift', *Friends Journal*, vol. 45, no. 7, 1999, pp. 8-10.

[37] H Alphonso, *The Personal Vocation*, 9th edn, Editrice Pontificia Universita Gregoriana, Rome, 2006.

[38] M McLennan, in *Meeting for Learning Resource Manual*, p. 8.

[39] H Bayes, *This We Can Say: Australian Quaker Life, Faith and Thought*, Australia Yearly Meeting of the Religious Society of Friends (Quakers) Inc., Armadale North, 2003, p. 98.

[40] D Lawson, *Meeting for Learning Resource Manual*, pp. 146-150.

[41] H Brinton, *Quaker Journals: Varieties of Religious Experience among Friends*, Pendle Hill Publishing, Wallingford, 1983.

[42] C Heywood, *Meeting for Learning Resource Manual*, p. 71.

[43] D Johnson, *Meeting for Learning Resource Manual*, p. 178.

[44] M Dwyer, *Praying Personally*, St Pauls Publications, Strathfield, 1998.

[45] W Davidson, *Meeting for Learning Resource Manual*, p. 11.

[46] C Jung, (1962) *Memories, Dreams and Reflections*, Pantheon, New York, 1962.

[47] D Lawson, *Mystical Meadows*, p. 117.

[48] D Lawson, *Mystical Meadows*, p. 132.

[49] H Bonar, 'Words to Winner of Souls' in *Celtic Daily Prayer A Northumbrian Office,* Compiled by A Raine and JT Skinner of the Northumbria Community, Harper Collins Publishers, London, 1984, p. 91.

www.ingramcontent.com/pod-product-compliance
Ingram Content Group UK Ltd.
Pitfield, Milton Keynes, MK11 3LW, UK
UKHW020230250726
13967UKWH00001B/290

9 781922 332233